Sanjeev Kapoor's

WRAP N ROLL

PopulaR
prakashan

www.popularprakashan.com

Sanjeev Kapoor's

WRAP N ROLL

In association with Alyona Kapoor

PopulaR prakashan

www.popularprakashan.com

Author's Note

The earliest wrap I remember eating is the roti sabzi in my lunch box in school! I never had the time to eat in the break, so my mother would take the sabzi and roll it up in a roti or parantha. This was just perfect for an active child to munch on while fooling around with friends during recess at school.

Things have not changed much. My wife Alyona packs the same roti sabzi for our daughters. Yes, there is this little bit of aluminium foil to cover the roll and there are a lot of variations in coverings and the stuffing, but then again, ours is a foodies' home!

Wrap n Roll gives you numerous options for snacks that are healthy, that take away the 'junk' from junk food and that give you a taste of foreign cuisine. There are also several options that are so filling they are mini-meals in themselves.

You will realise that a lot of creative thinking has gone into making the collection of recipes as varied as they are. For vegetarians, there are Baked Corn Rolls, Manchurian Rolls and more. Non-vegetarians can choose from Shawarma, Seafood Spring Rolls and many others.

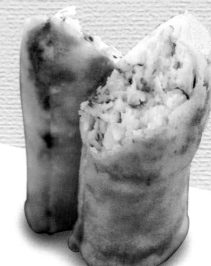

For weight watchers, the Salad Wraps and the Ratatouille Wraps are just perfect and the Satay Wraps or the Santa Fé Wraps are for those who do not mind eating and then burning it all off.

For party lovers, the Tortilla Rolls are lovely make-ahead starters. All one has to do is cut it up into small bite-sized pieces and serve with toothpicks. For those who prefer the crunch of deep-fried food with ketchup, there are Sago-Potato Rolls and Vegetable Rolls!

All the recipes will make four portions and this has to be kept in mind while planning the meal.

Happy Cooking!

CONTENTS

VEGETARIAN   (8-61)

Manchurian Rolls.................................9

Bread Rolls...10

Sago-Potato Rolls............................12

Cheese Calzones...............................13

Baked Corn Rolls..............................14

Cabbage Rolls....................................17

Cheesy Spinach Rolls.......................18

Vegetable Frankies...........................21

Middle-Eastern Wraps.....................22

Vegetable Spring Rolls.....................24

Tortilla Rolls......................................26

Teriyaki Rolls.....................................29

Vegetable Rolls..................................30

Satay Wraps.......................................33

Potato Rolls..34

Corn and Bean Burritos...................37

Spicy Moroccan Wraps....................38

Garden Wraps....................................40

Spiral Snack Rolls.............................41

Vegetable Papad Rolls......................42

Oriental Wraps..................................45

Paneer Tikka Kathi Rolls..................46

Ratatouille Wraps.............................49

Quesadillas..50

Paneer Wraps....................................53

Santa Fé Wraps..................................54

Pizza Margherita Wraps...................57

Salad Wraps....................................... 58

Stir-Fried Vegetable Wraps..............61

Non-Vegetarian (62-95)

Masala Keema Rolls.............................63

Chicken Wraps.............................64

Hot Dog Bowls.............................66

Creamy Chicken and
Vegetable Pancakes.............................67

Chicken Mole in Burritos.................68

Chicken Calzones.............................71

Fresh Rice Paper Rolls
with Prawns.............................72

Hot Dogs.............................73

Chicken Pita Pockets.....................75

Mushroom and Leek Spring Rolls......76

Sausage Triangles.............................77

Keema Roti Rolls.............................79

Chilli-Chicken Croissants.................80

Chicken Rolls.............................81

Omelette Rolls with
Sprouts and Sev.............................83

Mince Hot Dog Rolls.........................84

Seekh Roti.............................87

Shawarma.............................88

Moussaka Crêpes.............................91

Seafood Spring Rolls.....................92

Mutton Frankies.............................95

Desserts (96-101)

Mawa Rolls.............................96

Swiss Rolls.............................97

Boondi and Rabdi-
Stuffed Pancakes.............................98

Oat Pancakes with Dried Fruit..........99

Chocolate Pancakes with
Exotic Fruit 100

Cinnamon Rolls.............................101

ANNEXURE.............................102

GLOSSARY.............................103

MANCHURIAN ROLLS

Call it fusion or call it functional...but Chinese food with bread is pure innovation!

 Ingredients

 Method

4 crusty bread rolls

1 medium cabbage, grated

1 medium carrot, grated

¼ small cauliflower, grated

3 medium spring onions with greens, chopped

¼ cup refined flour

¼ cup cornflour

Salt to taste

Oil for deep-frying

Sauce

2 tablespoons oil

1-inch fresh ginger, chopped

4-6 garlic cloves, chopped

2-inch celery stalk, chopped

3 green chillies, chopped

2 tablespoons light soy sauce

1 teaspoon sugar

¼ teaspoon MSG (optional)

1 cup Vegetable Stock (see alongside)

2 tablespoons cornflour

1 tablespoon white vinegar

Salt to taste

- Mix the cabbage, carrot and cauliflower in a bowl and thoroughly rub in one teaspoon of salt. Add the spring onions, refined flour and cornflour. Mix thoroughly. Shape into lemon-sized balls.

- Heat sufficient oil in a wok and deep-fry the vegetable balls in small batches over a medium heat for three to four minutes or until golden brown. Drain on absorbent paper.

- For the sauce, heat two tablespoons of oil in a wok or a pan and stir-fry the ginger and garlic for one minute. Add the celery and green chillies and stir-fry for one minute longer.

- Add the soy sauce, sugar, MSG and salt to taste. Stir in the vegetable stock and bring to a boil.

- Mix two tablespoons of cornflour with half a cup of water and stir into the hot stock. Cook, stirring continuously, for a couple of minutes or until the sauce starts to thicken.

- Add the fried vegetable balls and vinegar and mix well.

- Slit open the rolls and fill with the vegetable balls and sauce. Serve immediately.

Note: For the Vegetable Stock, peel, wash and chop 1 onion, ½ a medium carrot, a 3-inch stalk celery and 2-3 garlic cloves. Place in a pan with 1 bay leaf, 5-6 peppercorns, 2-3 cloves and five cups of water and bring to a boil. Lower heat and simmer for fifteen minutes and strain. Cool and store in a refrigerator till further use.

BREAD ROLLS

A treat for cheese lovers with a yummy stuffing in the crusty roll.

 Ingredients

8 large slices of bread, crusts removed

1½ cups grated mozzarella cheese

1 medium onion, finely chopped

3 tablespoons chopped fresh coriander

1 green chilli, finely chopped

Salt to taste

Oil for deep-frying

To serve

Mint Chutney (page 102)

 Method

- In a bowl, combine the mozzarella cheese, onion, fresh coriander, green chilli and salt.

- Soak the slices of bread, one at a time, in water for about ten seconds. Squeeze out the excess water by gently pressing between your palms.

- Place each slice on the worktop, place some of the cheese mixture at one end and roll the bread up firmly to cover the stuffing completely, ensuring that the edges are well sealed.

- Heat sufficient oil in a deep pan and deep-fry the rolls until golden brown. Drain on absorbent paper.

- Serve hot with tomato ketchup or mint chutney.

SAGO-POTATO ROLLS

Serve these piping hot with chai...and rest assured that teatime will be highly enjoyable.

Ingredients

¾ cup sago

3 large potatoes, boiled and mashed

½ cup roasted and peeled peanuts, crushed

3 green chillies, chopped

1 inch ginger, chopped

1 tablespoon lemon juice

2-3 tablespoons chopped fresh coriander

Salt to taste

Oil for deep-frying

To serve

Green Chutney
(page 102)

Method

- Wash the sago and soak in water for at least one hour. If in a hurry, soak the sago in hot water till they swell. Squeeze out and place in a large bowl.

- Add the potatoes, peanuts, green chillies, ginger, lemon juice, fresh coriander and salt and mix well. Add a little water if necessary and make a dough. Let it stand for a few minutes.

- Divide the dough into eight equal portions and shape into oval rolls.

- Heat sufficient oil in a *kadai* till medium hot. Slide in four rolls at a time and deep-fry till golden brown. Drain on absorbent paper.

- Serve hot with green chutney.

Note: For a non-vegetarian version, you can substitute cooked minced meat (keema) for the mashed potatoes.

CHEESE CALZONES

A fusion packet...herbs have a way with paneer!
Or is it vice-versa?

 Ingredients

 Method

Pastry

1¼ cups refined flour

10 grams fresh yeast

¼ cup butter

Salt to taste

Filling

150 grams cottage cheese

2 tablespoons olive oil

4 garlic cloves, chopped

2 medium onions, chopped

½ cup Tomato Concasse
(page 71)

½ teaspoon red chilli flakes

½ teaspoon dried
mixed herbs

1 jalapeño chilli, chopped

3-4 black peppercorns,
crushed

Salt to taste

- Mix yeast with one tablespoon of lukewarm water and set aside for about ten minutes or till it froths.

- Sift refined flour and salt into a bowl. Make a well in the centre and pour in the yeast mixture. Add butter and sufficient water to knead the mixture into a soft, smooth dough. Cover the dough with a damp cloth and set aside in a warm place for about thirty minutes, or till it doubles in size.

- Preheat the oven to 200°C/400°F/Gas Mark 6. Grease a baking tray.

- Knock back the dough lightly, divide into four equal portions and roll out each portion into one-inch thick rounds. Set aside for about twenty minutes in a warm place.

- For the filling, heat olive oil in a pan. Add garlic and sauté for one minute. Add onions and continue to sauté till translucent.

- Stir in tomato concasse and cook till well-blended. Add the chilli flakes, mixed herbs, jalapeño chilli, salt and crushed peppercorns.

- Add the cottage cheese, mix well and set aside to cool.

- Divide the mixture into four portions and spread each portion over a pastry round. Fold over into a half-moon shape. Press the edges together to seal and place on the greased tray.

- Bake in the preheated oven for about forty-five minutes or till golden brown. Brush with melted butter and serve hot.

BAKED CORN ROLLS

This baked roll is not only delicious but also healthy since it is oil-free! For a party, you could make them smaller if you wish.

 Ingredients

12 slices of bread with the crusts removed

1 cup boiled sweetcorn

1 large potato, boiled and mashed

2 green chillies, chopped

1 teaspoon ginger paste

¼ cup chopped fresh coriander

1 teaspoon lemon juice

Salt to taste

2 tablespoons oil

1 large onion, chopped

To serve

Green Chutney (page 102)

 Method

- Preheat the oven to 180°C/350°F/ Gas Mark 4.

- Coarsely crush the boiled sweetcorn in a blender. Transfer into a bowl.

- Add the potato, green chillies, ginger paste, fresh coriander, lemon juice and salt and mix well.

- Heat the oil in a pan and sauté the onion till light brown. Add to the corn mixture and mix well. Divide the mixture into twelve equal portions and shape each one into an oval and set aside.

- Soak the slices of bread, one at a time, in water for about ten seconds. Squeeze out the excess water by gently pressing each slice between your palms. Place a potato-corn oval at one end of each slice and roll firmly to enclose the oval completely.

- Place the rolls on a greased baking tray. Bake for approximately twelve minutes or till the rolls turn light brown.

- Serve hot with tomato ketchup or green chutney.

CABBAGE ROLLS

Pakoras with a difference! This never fails to surprise family and friends.

 Ingredients

8 cabbage leaves

4 medium potatoes, boiled and mashed

½ cup green peas, boiled and mashed

1 teaspoon *chaat masala*

1 cup gram flour

½ teaspoon red chilli powder

½ teaspoon soda bicarbonate

Salt to taste

Oil for deep-frying

To serve

Mint Chutney (page 102)

 Method

· Blanch the cabbage leaves in boiling salted water. Drain and pat dry with absorbent paper.

· Mix the potatoes, green peas, salt and *chaat masala* in a bowl. Divide the mixture into eight equal portions.

· Place each portion of the mixture at one end of each cabbage leaf. Fold the sides around the filling and roll up the leaves firmly.

· Make a batter of coating consistency with the gram flour, chilli powder, salt, soda bicarbonate and some water.

· Heat sufficient oil in a *kadai*. Dip the cabbage rolls in the batter and deep-fry until golden brown. Drain on absorbent paper.

· Serve hot with tomato ketchup or mint chutney.

CHEESY SPINACH ROLLS

Fun way to have spinach and roti...yes,
even children will like this!

 Ingredients

¼ cup grated processed cheese

2 medium bunches (700 grams) spinach, blanched and chopped

1½ cups wholewheat flour

2 garlic cloves, chopped

2 green chillies, finely chopped

½ teaspoon *garam masala* powder

Salt to taste

3 tablespoons oil + for shallow-frying

 Method

- Mix the flour with salt and two tablespoons of oil. Add
  sufficient water and knead to make a soft dough. Divide into
  four portions and roll out each portion into a thin *chapati*. Heat
  a *tawa*, roast the *chapati* lightly and set aside.

- For the filling, heat one tablespoon of oil in a pan. Add the
  garlic and sauté for a minute. Add the spinach, green chillies,
  salt and *garam masala* powder, and mix well.

- Heat each *chapati* on a *tawa*. Spread half the spinach mixture
  over it and top with half the cheese. Place another *chapati* on
  top. Drizzle a little oil all around and cook for a few minutes.
  Flip over and drizzle a little more oil all around. Cook till both
  sides are evenly golden brown and crisp.

- Cut into wedges and serve hot.

VEGETABLE FRANKIES

Spicy, tangy, this mouth-watering snack is a favourite of many.

 Ingredients

4 refined flour *roti*

1 medium carrot, grated

¼ cup shelled green peas, parboiled and crushed

2 large potatoes, boiled and mashed

½ teaspoon cumin seeds

½ inch ginger, finely chopped

1 green chilli, finely chopped

¼ teaspoon red chilli powder

A pinch of turmeric powder

¼ teaspoon *garam masala* powder

1 tablespoon chopped fresh coriander

½ teaspoon dried mango powder

Salt to taste

1 tablespoon oil + for shallow-frying

To serve

4 teaspoons Green Chutney (page 102)

1 medium onion, sliced

1 teaspoon vinegar

Chaat masala to taste

 Method

- Heat one tablespoon oil in a non-stick pan; add the cumin seeds and sauté lightly. Add the carrot, green peas, ginger, green chilli, chilli powder, turmeric powder, *garam masala* powder and salt, and sauté over medium heat for two minutes. Transfer to a plate and cool.

- Add the mashed potatoes, fresh coriander and dried mango powder to the cooled mixture and mix well. Adjust seasoning.

- Divide the mixture into eight portions and shape into four-inch long cylinders. Shallow-fry the rolls in sufficient hot oil till pale gold. Drain on absorbent paper and set aside.

- To prepare the frankies, place each *roti* on a flat working surface and spread a teaspoon of green chutney all over the *roti*. Place a potato roll on one side. Sprinkle some of the sliced onions, drizzle one-fourth teaspoon of vinegar, sprinkle *chaat masala* over and roll up firmly.

- Wrap in aluminium foil and serve immediately.

MIDDLE-EASTERN WRAPS

Char-grilled veggies with rich tahini...the perfect combination secured in a homely roti.

 Ingredients

4 wholewheat *roti*

1½ teaspoons *tahini*

½ cup yogurt

5-6 fresh mint, roughly torn

1 medium onion, quartered

½ medium zucchini, sliced

1 medium carrot, sliced

1 medium green capsicum, cut into thick strips

2 teaspoons lemon juice

1 teaspoon mixed dried herbs

1 teaspoons red chilli flakes

A few sprigs of fresh parsley, chopped

Salt to taste

3 tablespoons olive oil

 Method

- Mix the *tahini*, yogurt, salt and fresh mint in a small bowl and set aside.

- Marinate the onion, zucchini, carrot and capsicum in a mixture of olive oil, lemon juice, mixed herbs, chilli flakes and salt for about fifteen minutes.

- Grill the vegetables on a hot grill till the grill marks are seen on the pieces. Remove and divide into four portions.

- To assemble the rolls, spread the *tahini* mixture on each *roti*, top with a portion of vegetables, sprinkle with parsley and roll up tightly.

- Serve immediately.

VEGETABLE SPRING ROLLS

Why not make the wrappers at home?
This recipe shows you how…

Ingredients

Spring roll wrappers

1 cup + 3 tablespoons cornflour

¼ cup refined flour

Salt to taste

Oil for deep-frying

Filling

1 medium onion, thinly sliced

2 medium carrots, grated

1 medium green capsicum, cut into thin strips

½ small cabbage, finely shredded

1 tablespoon light soy sauce

¼ teaspoon white pepper powder

¾ cup bean sprouts

2 spring onions with greens, finely sliced

Salt to taste

2 tablespoons oil

 Method

- To make the filling, heat two tablespoons of oil in a wok, add the onion and carrots and stir-fry for half a minute. Add the capsicum and cabbage and continue to stir-fry for one minute. Add the soy sauce, white pepper powder and salt.

- Add the bean sprouts and spring onions with the greens and stir-fry for about half a minute. Remove from heat and cool the filling to room temperature.

- To make the spring roll wrappers, mix one cup of cornflour, refined flour and salt to taste in a mixing bowl. Add two cups of water and whisk thoroughly. Strain the batter and set aside for fifteen minutes. Adjust the consistency of the batter by adding a little water if required.

- Heat an eight-inch non-stick frying pan, brush with a little oil and pour a ladleful of batter into it. Swirl to coat the bottom of the pan and pour the excess batter back into the bowl. Cook over medium heat till the edges start curling. Peel off or remove in one swift motion. Cool and sprinkle with a little cornflour. Repeat the process to make eight to ten wrappers.

- Mix one tablespoon of cornflour and two tablespoons of water to make a paste.

- Divide filling into eight to ten equal portions. Place a portion of filling at one end of each wrapper and roll up tightly, folding the sides in while you roll. Seal the ends with the cornflour paste.

- Heat sufficient oil in a wok; deep-fry two spring rolls at a time turning frequently, till crisp and golden brown. Drain on absorbent paper.

- Cut each spring roll into four pieces and serve hot with Sichuan Sauce (page 102).

TORTILLA ROLLS

Best served a little chilled, these rolls are splendid when you need to keep food ready in advance.

 Ingredients

4 ten-inch wholewheat tortillas

3 tablespoons cream cheese

¼ cup yogurt

1 teaspoon red chilli sauce

1 small red capsicum, finely chopped

1 small green capsicum, finely chopped

¼ cup sweetcorn kernels, boiled

1 medium onion, chopped

1 teaspoon lemon juice

1 tablespoon chopped fresh coriander

2-3 garlic cloves, finely chopped

Salt to taste

 Method

· In a bowl, mix together the cream cheese, yogurt, red chilli sauce, red capsicum, green capsicum, sweetcorn, onion, salt, lemon juice, fresh coriander and garlic. Divide the mixture into four equal portions.

· Place each tortilla on the worktop, spread one portion of the mixture evenly over it and roll up tightly. Wrap in foil and place in a refrigerator to chill for half an hour.

· When ready to serve, remove the foil and slice each roll diagonally into two-inch thick slices and serve chilled.

Note: You can use cooked chicken or chicken tikka cut into small pieces for a non-vegetarian version.

TERIYAKI ROLLS

A taste of Japanese splendour…in a handy tofu-filled roll.

 Ingredients

4 medium crusty bread rolls

2 medium green capsicums, sliced

10 fresh button mushrooms, sliced

1 large onion, sliced

½ cup tofu cubes

1 tablespoon olive oil

Teriyaki sauce

2 tablespoons butter

1 inch ginger, sliced

1 medium onion, finely chopped

½ cup white wine

12-15 black grapes, roughly crushed by hand

1 tablespoon soy sauce

½ teaspoon black pepper powder

1 tablespoon molasses

2 tablespoons honey

Salt to taste

 Method

- To make the teriyaki sauce, heat the butter in a pan. Add the ginger and onion and sauté till golden brown.

- Add the white wine and cook till the mixture reduces a little.

- Add the crushed black grapes and continue to cook, stirring, for five to seven minutes till the grapes are soft.

- Add the soy sauce, pepper powder, salt, molasses and honey. Mix well and strain.

- Heat the olive oil in a pan; add the capsicums, mushrooms, onion and tofu and toss for two minutes.

- Stir in the teriyaki sauce and cook for two minutes. Divide the mixture into four portions.

- Cut the crusty rolls in half and spread one portion of the vegetable and tofu mixture on one half of each roll and cover with the other half.

- Serve immediately.

VEGETABLE ROLLS

Crisp crust with tender vegetables inside...
just ensure that you don't run out of ketchup!

 Ingredients

10-12 French beans, finely chopped

2 medium carrots, finely chopped

2 large potatoes, finely chopped

½ teaspoon *garam masala* powder

1½ teaspoons red chilli powder

1¼ teaspoons dried mango powder

4 bread slices

50 grams semolina

Green Chutney (page 102)

Salt to taste

2 tablespoons oil + for deep-frying

 Method

- Heat two tablespoons of oil in a pan and sauté the French beans, carrots and potatoes till all the moisture evaporates and the vegetables are slightly tender.

- Mash them slightly while hot. Add the *garam masala* powder, chilli powder, dried mango powder and salt. Mix well.

- Soak the bread slices in water for a couple of seconds and then squeeze out thoroughly. Add to the vegetables. Mix well and shape into long thick rolls.

- Heat sufficient oil in a *kadai*. Coat the rolls with the semolina and deep-fry over medium heat till golden brown and crisp. Drain on absorbent paper.

- Serve hot with green chutney.

Satay Wraps

Take time off to make this, involve the kids too and enjoy a wrap that is worth all the effort.

 ## Ingredients

2 cups tofu cubes

1 red capsicum, sliced

1 zucchini, sliced

7-8 fresh button mushrooms, sliced

5-6 slices of tinned pineapple, quartered

2 garlic cloves, sliced

½ cup bean sprouts

1 tablespoon olive oil

Pancake batter

1 cup refined flour

¼ cup milk

A pinch of salt

4 teaspoons oil + for greasing

Satay sauce

¼ cup roasted peanuts, coarsely powdered

4 garlic cloves, chopped

1 small onion, grated

½ teaspoon red chilli powder

1 tablespoon dark soy sauce

3 tablespoons tomato purée

2 teaspoons honey

Salt to taste

1 teaspoon oil

 ## Method

· Preheat the oven to 180°C/350°F/Gas Mark 4.

· To make the satay sauce, heat the oil in a pan and add the garlic and onion. Sauté over high heat, for half a minute.

· Add the chilli powder and then immediately add the dark soy sauce, tomato purée, honey, crushed peanuts, salt and one cup of water.

· Bring the mixture to a boil and simmer for five minutes, stirring occasionally. Remove from heat and set aside.

· To make the pancake batter, blend together the flour, a pinch of salt, milk and water as required and whisk well so that no lumps form. Add four teaspoons of oil and whisk till smooth.

· Lightly grease a frying pan and heat till moderately hot. Pour a ladleful of batter and rotate the pan to spread it evenly. Cook till done. Similarly make the remaining pancakes.

· Generously apply the satay sauce with a pastry brush to the tofu, capsicum, zucchini, mushrooms and pineapple pieces.

· Roast in the oven for about twenty minutes, turning occasionally. Meanwhile sauté the garlic in olive oil until fragrant.

· Place the roasted vegetables and tofu on the pancakes. Top with bean sprouts and fried garlic. Roll up the pancakes tightly.

· Slice each pancake into several pieces and serve with the remaining satay sauce.

POTATO ROLLS

It is worthwhile to surprise your guests with these stuffed rolls…and take my tip, make plenty of these!

 Ingredients

4 large potatoes, boiled and mashed

4 bread slices

½ teaspoon black pepper powder

10 cashew nuts, coarsely pounded

2 green chillies, finely chopped

1 inch ginger, finely chopped

½ cup shelled green peas, blanched and coarsely ground

2 tablespoons chopped fresh coriander

Tomato ketchup, as required

Salt to taste

¼ cup *ghee* + for shallow-frying

 Method

- Crumble the bread to make fine breadcrumbs. Mix with the potatoes, salt and pepper powder to make a dough. Divide into eight equal portions.

- Grease your palm with *ghee* and roll the dough into balls.

- Mix together the pounded cashew nuts, green chillies, ginger, green peas, fresh coriander and salt. Divide into eight equal portions.

- Take each potato ball in your palm and make a hollow in it. Place a portion of the cashew nut stuffing in the centre and gather the edges together to cover the stuffing. Shape into an oblong roll.

- Heat sufficient *ghee* in a flat frying pan. Lower heat and place four rolls at a time on it. Shallow-fry till the rolls are evenly golden brown on all sides. Drain on absorbent paper.

- Serve hot with tomato ketchup.

CORN AND BEAN BURRITOS

Warm to the core and filling to the last bite, these burritos make you a perfect early dinner.

 Ingredients

100 grams sweetcorn kernels

250 grams sprouted beans, blanched

4 refined flour tortillas

½ cup grated mozzarella cheese

10-12 black peppercorns, crushed

1 tablespoon lemon juice

1 medium tomato, chopped

½ cup shredded lettuce

2 spring onions, chopped

2 green chillies, chopped

½ cup Salsa (page 54)

Salt to taste

Chilled sour cream, to serve

 Method

- Preheat the oven to 200°C/400°F/Gas Mark 6.

- Mix the cheese, salt, crushed peppercorns, lemon juice and sprouted beans in a bowl.

- In another bowl, mix together the tomato, lettuce and spring onions thoroughly. Add the corn and green chillies and mix.

- Place the tortillas on a plate. Layer equal portions of the cheese and bean mixture and the corn and tomato mixture on each tortilla. Sprinkle the salsa on top and fold each tortilla over.

- Arrange the tortillas in a baking dish and bake for twenty minutes.

- Serve hot with the chilled sour cream.

SPICY MOROCCAN WRAPS

Take a hint from the name…it's spicy…if you can't take it, reduce the number of chillies.

 Ingredients

4 cornmeal (page 50) or wholewheat tortillas

1 large green zucchini, cut into ½-inch cubes

2 medium yellow capsicums, cut into ½-inch squares

¼ teaspoon red chilli flakes

¼ teaspoon black pepper powder

¼ teaspoon mixed dried herbs

10-12 chopped green or black olives

½ cup sun-dried tomatoes, soaked in water and chopped

1 tablespoon chopped fresh parsley

Salt to taste

2 tablespoons olive oil

Harrisa sauce

6 dried red chillies

1 teaspoon coriander seeds

1 teaspoon caraway seeds

1 teaspoon cumin seeds

1 garlic clove, minced

1 tablespoon vinegar

Salt to taste

 Method

- To make the harrisa sauce, soak the red chillies in one cup of water for ten minutes.

- Dry-roast the coriander seeds, caraway seeds and cumin seeds till fragrant and grind them with the red chillies. Transfer the mixture to a bowl, add the garlic, vinegar and salt and mix well.

- Preheat the oven to 180°C/350°F/Gas Mark 4.

- Marinate the zucchini and yellow capsicums in a mixture of olive oil, chilli flakes, salt, pepper powder and mixed herbs for ten minutes.

- Roast the vegetables in the oven for twenty minutes.

- Add the olives, sun-dried tomatoes and parsley to the roasted vegetables and mix. Stir in the harrisa sauce.

- Spread the mixture equally over the tortillas and roll up firmly.

- Serve immediately.

GARDEN WRAPS

This quick, no-cook wrap is just right for those sudden hunger pangs!

 Ingredients

4 refined flour tortillas

½ cup cream cheese

1 cup shredded iceberg lettuce

1 medium onion, sliced

2 medium cucumbers, cut into thin strips

2 medium tomatoes, cut into thin strips

½ cup bean sprouts

1 teaspoon red chilli flakes

Salt to taste

 Method

· Spread the cream cheese on the tortillas.

· Top with the lettuce, onion, cucumbers, tomatoes and bean sprouts. Sprinkle the chilli flakes and salt on top.

· Roll up each tortilla tightly. Cut in half and serve immediately.

SPIRAL SNACK ROLLS

Freshly baked rolls bursting with spicy vegetables are perfect party fare!

 ## Ingredients

 ## Method

3 cups refined flour + for dusting

7 grams dry yeast

2 teaspoons sugar

30 grams butter

1½ teaspoons salt

Filling

3 medium potatoes, boiled and chopped

2 medium onions, chopped

2 medium tomatoes, chopped

½ cup green peas

½ teaspoon cumin seeds

1 teaspoon ginger paste

1 teaspoon garlic paste

2 green chillies, chopped

½ teaspoon red chilli powder

1 teaspoon *pav bhaji masala*

Salt to taste

2 tablespoons oil

- Sift flour and salt together into a bowl.

- Mix yeast and sugar in a small bowl. Add one-fourth cup of lukewarm water and set aside till it begins to froth.

- Add the yeast mixture to the flour and knead, adding water, a little at a time, till you use up one cup of water. Keep stretching the dough from time to time and kneading it till you get a smooth and elastic dough. Cover with a damp cloth and set it aside in a warm place till it doubles in size.

- For the filling, heat oil in a pan, add cumin seeds. When they begin to change colour add ginger, garlic, green chillies and onions and sauté till the onions are translucent.

- Add the tomatoes and green peas and sauté till peas are cooked. Add the chilli powder, *pav bhaji masala*, salt and potatoes and mix. Remove from heat and let it cool.

- Lightly dust the rolling pin with flour and roll the dough into a rectangle about thirty by sixty centimetres. Spread the filling evenly.

- Starting at the narrow end, roll the dough as tightly as you can towards the other end. Pinch the seam to seal it. Cut the roll diagonally into eight equal pieces.

- Grease a large baking tray. Arrange the pieces, cut side down, in the tray. Cover tightly with a cling film. Place in a warm place for about one-and-a-half hours or till the pieces double in size.

- Preheat oven 190°C/375°F/Gas Mark 5.

- Place the baking tray in the preheated oven and bake for twenty-five to thirty minutes. The rolls should be golden brown yet very soft to touch.

- Once done, remove and brush with melted butter and leave them on a wire rack to cool. Slice on the slant and serve.

VEGETABLE PAPAD ROLLS

Best served as soon as they are off the heat, these rolls are excellent starters with drinks and mocktails.

 Ingredients

8 medium *urad papads*

1 medium carrot, chopped

1 medium potato, chopped

6 French beans, chopped

100 grams cauliflower, chopped

1 tomato, chopped

½ teaspoon turmeric powder

½ teaspoon red chilli powder

1 tablespoon chopped fresh coriander

Salt to taste

1 tablespoon oil + for deep-frying

 Method

· Boil the carrot, potato, French beans and cauliflower with a pinch of salt till three-fourth cooked. Drain water and spread the vegetables out to dry.

· Heat one tablespoon of oil in a pan and sauté the tomato. Add the boiled vegetables and sauté for a while. Add the turmeric powder and chilli powder and mix well. Add the fresh coriander, remove from heat and set aside to cool.

· Dip each *papad* in water so that it becomes pliable. Spoon a little mixture along the centre and roll the *papad* up like a dosa. Press the ends well to seal.

· Heat sufficient oil in a *kadai* till it starts smoking. Deep-fry the *papad* rolls on both sides till crisp. Drain on absorbent paper.

· Serve hot.

ORIENTAL WRAPS

Simple tofu glorified with sesame dressing...with pita as a perfect foil.

 Ingredients

2 pita breads

1 cup tofu cubes

Chilli-garlic sauce, as required

½ cup shredded red cabbage

½ cup shredded carrot

2 spring onions with greens, sliced

Sesame dressing

2 tablespoon roasted sesame seeds

¼ inch ginger

1 garlic clove

1 tablespoon soy sauce

2 tablespoons rice wine vinegar

2 teaspoons sugar

Salt to taste

 Method

- For the dressing, powder the sesame seeds in a blender. Add the ginger and garlic and blend for half a minute. Add the soy sauce, rice wine vinegar, salt and sugar and blend some more. If the mixture is too thick, add a little water. Transfer the dressing to a bowl.

- Preheat the oven to 200°C/400°F/Gas Mark 6.

- Marinate the tofu cubes in two tablespoons of sesame dressing for fifteen minutes.

- Place the tofu on a baking sheet and bake for thirty minutes. Reserve the remaining dressing. Take the tofu out of the oven and set aside to cool.

- Spread the chilli-garlic sauce on each pita bread. Place a layer each of red cabbage and carrots and spring onions with greens on top. Arrange the baked tofu over the vegetables.

- Drizzle the remaining dressing over the tofu. Roll up and cut each pita bread into half.

- Serve immediately.

PANEER TIKKA KATHI ROLLS

Spicy soft paneer in even softer chapati...your family is going to love this recipe.

 Ingredients

 Method

Filling

1 cup low-fat cottage cheese, cut into ½-inch cubes

2 medium tomatoes, seeded and chopped

1 teaspoon oil

2 medium green capsicums, chopped

Marinade

¼ cup yogurt, whisked

1 teaspoon red chilli powder

¼ teaspoon turmeric powder

½ teaspoon ginger paste

¼ teaspoon garlic paste

1 tablespoon gram flour

½ teaspoon *chaat masala*

½ teaspoon dried fenugreek leaves

½ teaspoon *garam masala* powder

Salt to taste

Chapati

1 cup wholewheat flour

¼ cup skimmed milk

Salt to taste

- Mix together all the ingredients for the marinade in a deep bowl. Add the cottage cheese and tomatoes and toss lightly. Set aside to marinate for ten minutes.

- Heat the oil in a non-stick pan. Add the green capsicums and sauté for two minutes.

- Add the cottage cheese mixture and sauté over high heat for four to five minutes, stirring occasionally. Cook till dry and set aside.

- For the *chapati*, combine all the ingredients and knead into soft dough. Divide the dough into eight equal portions. Roll out each portion into a thin *chapati*.

- Heat a *tawa* and cook each *chapati* lightly on both sides. Set aside.

- Divide the *tikka* filling into eight equal portions.

- Place one portion of the filling in the centre of each *chapati* and roll up tightly.

- To serve, cook the rolls on a hot *tawa* till warm. Cut into two-inch long pieces and serve hot.

RATATOUILLE WRAPS

Handy way to pocket some fresh vegetables…and label it international too!

 Ingredients

4 pita breads

2 medium onions, chopped

2 garlic cloves, finely chopped

1 red capsicum, cut into
½-inch squares

2 small zucchini, cut into
½-inch cubes

3 small brinjals, chopped

2 tomatoes, chopped

1 tablespoon chopped fresh parsley

Black pepper powder to taste

¼ teaspoon paprika flakes

¼ teaspoon dried oregano

Salt to taste

2 tablespoons olive oil

 Method

- To make the ratatouille, heat the olive oil in a pan. Add the onions and garlic and sauté for five minutes or until soft. Add the capsicum, zucchini and brinjals and cook for five more minutes. Add the tomatoes and half a cup of water.

- Cover the pan and cook for fifteen minutes. Uncover occasionally and stir gently. Add the parsley during the last three to four minutes of cooking.

- Add the salt, pepper powder, paprika flakes and oregano and mix well.

- Cut each pita bread in half and open out the pocket.

- Spoon the ratatouille into the pita pockets and serve immediately.

QUESADILLAS

A touch of easy Mexican for your daily menu. Another plus point – it's really nutritious.

 Ingredients

 Method

Tortillas

1 cup cornmeal

½ cup refined flour

¼ cup milk

Salt to taste

Filling

2 medium onions, chopped

6-8 garlic cloves, chopped

2 cups kidney beans, boiled

6 tablespoons tomato ketchup

4 green chillies, chopped

2 teaspoons paprika

2 cups grated processed cheese

4 tablespoons fresh coriander, chopped

Salt to taste

2 tablespoons olive oil

- Mix together the cornmeal, refined flour and salt. Knead into a soft dough with milk and half a cup of water. Cover with a damp piece of muslin and set aside for a few minutes.

- Divide the dough into eight equal portions and roll out each portion into a thin ten-inch round tortilla (*chapati*). Lightly cook each tortilla on both sides on a hot *tawa* and set aside.

- To make the filling, heat one tablespoon of olive oil in a pan and sauté the onions and garlic for one minute.

- Add the boiled kidney beans, tomato ketchup, green chillies, paprika and salt and cook for two to three minutes.

- To make the quesadillas, heat a *tawa* and place a tortilla on it. Spread one-fourth portion of the filling, and top with one-fourth portion of the cheese and fresh coriander. Cover with another tortilla. Drizzle some olive oil all around.

- Turn the tortilla over gently when the underside has cooked. Cook the other side.

- Remove, cut into wedges and serve hot.

PANEER WRAPS

Even a dieter will be able to enjoy this...just skimp on the oil to make it even lighter.

 Ingredients

300 grams cottage cheese, cut into ½-inch cubes

4 wholewheat flour *roomali roti*

2 tablespoons vinegar

2 green chillies, sliced

½ teaspoon garlic paste

½ teaspoon ginger paste

1 small onion, sliced

1 medium green capsicum, cut into thin strips

1 teaspoon red chilli powder

¼ teaspoon turmeric powder

1 teaspoon dried mango powder

½ cup bean sprouts

1 tablespoon *ghee*

4 large lettuce leaves

Salt to taste

2 tablespoons oil

 Method

- Combine the vinegar and green chillies in a bowl and set aside.

- Heat the oil in a pan; add the garlic paste and ginger paste and sauté for half a minute. Add the onion and continue to sauté for half a minute longer.

- Add the capsicum, chilli powder, turmeric powder, mango powder, salt and cottage cheese cubes and sauté over medium heat for two minutes.

- Add the bean sprouts and continue to sauté for another minute. Remove from heat and set aside.

- To prepare the wraps, divide the cottage cheese mixture into four equal portions. Place a *roomali roti* on the worktop and arrange a lettuce leaf over it. Spread a portion of cottage cheese mixture on the *roti*, drizzle half a teaspoon of the vinegar-chilli mixture, roll up and secure with aluminium foil.

- Serve immediately.

Santa Fé Wraps

Beans, cream and roasted corn…flavours and textures that make a simple wrap unforgettable.

 ## Ingredients

2 Corn Tortillas (page 50)

2 cups fresh corn kernels

1 zucchini, chopped

½ cup tinned black beans, mashed

¼ cup sour cream

½ cup grated processed cheese

Salt to taste

1 tablespoon olive oil

Salsa

2 large onions, halved

5 garlic cloves, halved

4 medium tomatoes, halved

1 green capsicum, quartered

1 tablespoon lemon juice

Salt to taste

 ## Method

- To make the salsa, place the onions, garlic, tomatoes and capsicum on a hot griddle and roast till the skins are charred.

- Cool and grind coarsely with salt. Transfer to a bowl and stir in the lemon juice. Set aside.

- Preheat the oven to 200°C/400°F/Gas Mark 6.

- Mix together the corn, zucchini, salt and olive oil in a bowl. Transfer the mixture to an ovenproof pan and roast it in the oven for fifteen minutes.

- Spread the mashed black beans over each tortilla. Spread a layer of sour cream on top. Arrange the roasted corn and zucchini over the sour cream.

- Spread the salsa and cheese on top of the corn-zucchini layer. Roll up the tortillas, cut each in half and serve immediately.

Pizza Margherita Wraps

A no-mess closed pizza that travels well in a lunch box!

 Ingredients

4 pita breads

1 cup pizza sauce

16 tomato slices

4 thick slices of mozzarella cheese

2 tablespoons shredded fresh basil

1 tablespoon olive oil

 Method

- Slice each pita bread vertically into two.

- Spread some pizza sauce on one slice. Arrange the tomato slices over the sauce followed by one slice of cheese.

- Sprinkle fresh basil and cover with the other slice of pita bread. Apply some olive oil on top of each slice. Grill until brown on both sides.

- Serve immediately.

SALAD WRAPS

Need to rustle up healthy food in a few minutes?
This wrap is made for just such a need!

 Ingredients

4 wholewheat tortillas

2 tablespoons balsamic vinegar

Black pepper powder to taste

2 cups roughly torn mixed lettuce
(lollo rosso, romaine and iceberg)

½ cup sweetcorn kernels, boiled

2 medium cucumbers, cubed

4 tablespoons sour cream

Salt to taste

4 tablespoons olive oil

 Method

- Combine the olive oil, vinegar, salt and pepper powder to make a vinaigrette dressing. Combine the lettuce, sweetcorn and cucumber with the vinaigrette.

- Heat the tortillas on a *tawa* for about twenty seconds. You can also heat them in a microwave oven.

- Spread the salad evenly on each warm tortilla, drizzle with sour cream and roll up.

- Serve immediately.

Stir-fried Vegetable Wraps

Translucent rice paper with crunchy filling and sweet sauce...transports you to the Orient.

 **Ingredients**

4 rice papers

2 spring onions, chopped

½ cup chopped water chestnuts

½ inch ginger, minced

2 tablespoons soy sauce

1 teaspoon red chilli sauce

1 tablespoon rice vinegar

½ cup bean sprouts

2 tablespoons plum sauce, for dipping

1 tablespoon oil

 Method

- Soak the rice papers in water for one minute before using.

- Heat the oil in a pan and stir-fry the spring onions and water chestnuts for about two minutes. Add the ginger, soy sauce, red chilli sauce and rice vinegar. Stir-fry for another two minutes ensuring that the vegetables remain crunchy and are not overcooked.

- Add the bean sprouts and stir-fry for another minute.

- Divide this mixture into four portions and place a portion on each rice paper. Roll up tightly.

- Serve immediately.

Masala Keema Rolls

Tasty keema with green chutney in fresh roti...
filling and fulfilling!

Ingredients

Method

Masala keema

500 grams minced mutton

¾ cup skimmed milk yogurt

1 tablespoon garlic paste

½ tablespoon ginger paste

1 teaspoon red chilli powder

½ teaspoon *garam masala* powder

8 teaspoons Green Chutney
(page 102)

1 teaspoon chilli sauce

1 teaspoon tomato sauce

2 medium onions, sliced into rings

2 tablespoons lemon juice

2 teaspoons *chaat masala*

Salt to taste

2 tablespoons oil

Roti

1½ cups wholewheat flour

3 tablespoons skimmed milk yogurt

Salt to taste

- Mix together the yogurt, garlic paste, ginger paste, chilli powder, *garam masala* powder and salt.

- Marinate the mutton mince in the mixture for thirty to forty minutes.

- Heat the oil in a pan. Add the marinated mince and cook over medium heat till the mince is cooked and dry. Divide into eight equal portions.

- In another bowl, mix together the wholewheat flour, yogurt and salt. Add sufficient water and knead into a soft dough. Cover the dough with a damp cloth and allow it to rest for eight to ten minutes.

- Divide the dough into eight equal portions. Roll out each portion into a seven-inch *roti*.

- Heat a *tawa*; place each *roti* on it and roast till brown specks appear on both sides.

- Spread a teaspoon of the green chutney on the *roti* and drizzle some chilli sauce and tomato sauce. Place one portion of the mince and some onion rings on the *roti*. Sprinkle lemon juice and *chaat masala* and roll up firmly.

- Serve immediately.

CHICKEN WRAPS

Look for some good quality pita for this...the crispy chicken adds character.

 Ingredients

2 (180 grams each) boneless chicken breasts

2 pita breads

2 tablespoons vinegar

1 tablespoon sugar

1 green chilli, chopped

1 small carrot, grated

1 small cabbage, shredded

1 small green capsicum, finely sliced

1 teaspoon ginger paste

1 teaspoon garlic paste

1 teaspoon cumin powder

1 teaspoon red chilli powder

1 tablespoon lemon juice

½ teaspoon soy sauce

1 egg, lightly beaten

¼ cup refined flour

¼ cup Mint Chutney (page 102)

1 medium onion, sliced into rings

Salt to taste

Oil for deep-frying

 Method

- In a bowl, mix the vinegar, sugar, salt and green chilli thoroughly. Leave to stand for about half an hour or till the vinegar becomes a little spicy; strain the vinegar. Add the carrot, cabbage and green capsicum to the strained vinegar and toss well. Chill in a refrigerator till required.

- Cut the chicken into strips. In a bowl, mix the ginger paste, garlic paste, cumin powder, chilli powder, lemon juice, soy sauce, salt and egg. Add the chicken and flour and mix thoroughly. Set aside to marinate for half an hour, preferably in a refrigerator.

- Heat plenty of oil in a *kadai*. Deep-fry the chicken till cooked. Drain on absorbent paper.

- Heat both sides of the pita breads on a *tawa* or in an oven.

- Cut each pita bread in half and open out the pockets. Spread some mint chutney on the inside of each half, and fill with a portion each of chicken, vegetable mixture and onion rings.

- Serve immediately.

HOT DOG BOWLS

Dive into the savoury centre and taste the cheesy meaty filling…simply yummy!

 Ingredients

3 small hot dog sausages, sliced

4 small hamburger buns

1 small onion, chopped

3-4 garlic cloves, chopped

¼ cup tomato sauce

1 cup cooked red kidney beans

6-8 black peppercorns, crushed

3 teaspoons butter

¼ cup grated processed cheese

Salt to taste

2 tablespoons oil

 Method

- Heat the oil in a pan over medium heat. Sauté the hot dogs till golden brown. Drain and set aside. Add the onion to the pan and sauté till golden brown. Add the garlic and sauté until pale gold.

- Add the tomato sauce and cook, stirring occasionally, for two minutes. Stir in the kidney beans, lower heat and simmer for four minutes. Stir in the hot dog sausages, salt and crushed peppercorns and simmer for another minute. Remove from heat. Divide into four equal portions.

- Cut the tops off the buns horizontally. Scoop out the centre of the buns, leaving about an inch around the sides to form a bread bowl. Lightly butter the insides of each bowl.

- Spoon one portion of the filling into each bowl and sprinkle with the grated cheese. Serve immediately.

CREAMY CHICKEN AND VEGETABLE PANCAKES

This recipe is wonderful for large brunch parties as the pancakes can be made in advance.

 ## Ingredients

 ## Method

Pancakes

½ cup wholewheat flour

2 eggs

¾ cup milk

Salt to taste

Oil for cooking

Filling

3 (450 grams) chicken breast fillets

1 small onion, sliced

1 sprig parsley, chopped

2 carrots, grated

½ teaspoon oregano

1 teaspoon mustard paste

1 teaspoon lemon juice

½ cup white wine

3 black peppercorns, crushed

1 tablespoon refined flour

½ cup milk

½ cup cream

1 teaspoon French mustard

Black pepper powder to taste

Salt to taste

2½ tablespoons olive oil

- Marinate the chicken breasts in a mixture of oregano, mustard paste, salt and lemon juice for fifteen minutes.

- For the pancakes, sift the flour in a bowl. Make a well in the centre and add eggs and work the flour from the sides. Gradually add the milk and whisk to make a smooth batter. Add the salt and mix again. Set aside to stand for thirty minutes.

- Heat one tablespoon of olive oil in a pan. Add the onion and sauté till transluscent. Add the marinated chicken and sear it. Add wine and half a cup of water and cook till the chicken is tender. Add parsley and crushed peppercorns and mix well. Remove the chicken onto a plate and reserve the juices.

- Heat one tablespoon olive oil in a pan. Stir in the flour, reserved juices, milk and cream and mix well ensuring that there are no lumps. Cook till the sauce comes to a boil. Remove from heat and add mustard, salt and pepper powder.

- Heat the remaining olive oil in another pan, add the carrot and stir-fry until just tender.

- Combine the chicken, sauce and carrots well. Heat a pan and grease it. Pour two to three tablespoons of batter and cook slowly until set and lightly browned underneath. Flip and cook till the other side is cooked similarly.

- Divide the filling evenly between the pancakes and roll up. Serve immediately.

Chicken Mole In Burritos

Rich creamy chicken filling in warm tortillas...perfect for a Sunday brunch!

 Ingredients

 Method

Ingredients

2 (250 grams) chicken breasts, boiled and shredded

4 wholewheat tortillas

2 medium onions, chopped

2 garlic cloves, minced

1 teaspoon dried oregano

½ teaspoon cinnamon powder

¾-inch ginger, grated

1 teaspoon red chilli powder

½ teaspoon clove powder

¼ teaspoon nutmeg powder

1 teaspoon cumin powder

1 cup Chicken Stock
(see alongside)

¼ cup tomato paste

2 tablespoons almond paste

Hot and sour tomato sauce to taste

Yogurt, as required

Salt to taste

2 teaspoons oil

Method

- Heat the oil in a pan and sauté the onions over medium heat till they turn soft. Add the garlic, oregano, cinnamon powder, ginger, chilli powder, clove powder, nutmeg powder and cumin powder and cook over medium heat for two minutes, stirring frequently.

- Add the chicken, chicken stock, tomato paste, almond paste and salt and bring the mixture to a boil. Simmer over medium heat, uncovered, for ten minutes till the mixture thickens. Add the hot and sour tomato sauce and mix.

- Warm the tortillas in a slow oven. Fill each tortilla with three-fourth cup of the chicken mixture and roll up. Cut diagonally in half and serve with the yogurt.

Note: For the Chicken Stock, boil 200 grams chicken bones in water for 5 minutes. Drain and discard water. Boil blanched bones with a roughly chopped carrot, celery stalk, leek, 2-3 parsley stalks, 6-7 black peppercorns, 5-6 cloves, 1 bay leaf and 10 cups of water. Remove any scum which rises to the surface and replace it with more cold water. Simmer for at least one hour. Remove from heat, strain, cool and store in a refrigerator till further use.
Unutilised chicken carcass (neck, winglets, bones etc.) can be used to make stock.

CHICKEN CALZONES

Nothing can be better than this finger food! I love making them in large batches for a party.

 Ingredients

 Method

Covering

2 cups refined flour

5 grams fresh yeast

½ teaspoon sugar

Butter as required

½ teaspoon salt

1 tablespoon olive oil

Filling

2 chicken breasts, chopped

4 garlic cloves, chopped

2 medium onions, chopped

1 medium green capsicum, chopped

½ cup Tomato Concasse (see alongside)

½ teaspoon red chilli flakes

½ teaspoon dried mixed herbs

1 jalapeño chilli, chopped

3-4 black peppercorns, crushed

Salt to taste

2 tablespoons olive oil

- For the covering, sift the refined flour with salt and make a well in the centre. Dissolve the yeast in lukewarm water along with some sugar and pour into the well. Mix.

- Make a soft dough using water as required. Cover with a damp cloth and set aside at room temperature till it doubles in size.

- Preheat the oven to 200°C/400°F/Gas Mark 6. Grease a baking tray with one tablespoon olive oil.

- Knock back the dough lightly, divide into four equal portions and roll out each portion into a one-inch thick round. Set aside for about twenty minutes in a warm place.

- For the filling, heat the olive oil in a pan; add the garlic and sauté for one minute. Add the onions and continue to sauté till translucent.

- Add the capsicum and chicken and sauté for three to four minutes. Stir in the tomato concasse and cook till well blended.

- Add the chilli flakes, mixed herbs, jalapeño chilli, salt and crushed peppercorns. Mix well, remove from heat and set aside to cool.

- Divide the mixture into four portions and spread each portion over a pastry round. Fold over into a half-moon shape. Press the edges together to seal and place on the greased tray.

- Bake for about forty-five minutes till golden brown. Brush with melted butter and serve hot.

Note: To make Tomato Concasse, blanch and peel four medium tomatoes, remove seeds and chop finely. Makes one cup.

FRESH RICE PAPER ROLLS WITH PRAWNS

As this starter is translucent, it has high visual appeal for seafood lovers.

Ingredients

24 medium prawns, shelled and deveined

12 rice paper rounds each measuring 16 centimetres

1 teaspoon garlic paste

Black pepper powder to taste

1 cup finely shredded cabbage

½ cup coarsely grated carrot

2 tablespoons coarsely chopped fresh mint

2 tablespoons coarsely chopped fresh coriander

Salt to taste

2 tablespoons oil

Dipping sauce

$1/_3$ cup caster sugar

¼ cup white vinegar

2 teaspoons fish sauce

2 fresh red chillies, sliced thinly

1 tablespoon finely chopped fresh coriander

Method

· Marinate the prawns in a mixture of garlic paste, salt and pepper powder for fifteen minutes.

· Heat the oil in a pan and toss the prawns till cooked. Set aside.

· Combine the cabbage, carrot, fresh mint and fresh coriander in a bowl.

· For the dipping sauce, heat sugar, vinegar and one-fourth cup of water in a small pan and stir until the sugar dissolves. Bring the mixture to a boil, remove from heat and add fish sauce and red chillies. Set aside to cool and add the fresh coriander.

· Soak the rice papers in water for one minute and place them on a serving plate.

· Divide the vegetable mixture equally into twelve portions and place in the centre of each round. Place two prawns over the vegetable mixture. Fold in the sides and roll to enclose the filling.

· Serve immediately with the dipping sauce.

Hot Dogs

As traditional as they come…hot dogs are eternal favourites.

Ingredients

4 bread rolls

4 chicken sausages

2 tablespoons butter

4 tablespoons Mayonnaise (page 102)

2 teaspoons mustard paste

Method

- Slit the bread rolls without cutting through.

- Heat the butter in a pan and sauté the chicken sausages for a minute. Drain and set aside.

- In the same pan, lightly warm the bread rolls.

- Place one sautéed sausage in each roll. Spread one tablespoon of mayonnaise and half a teaspoon of mustard paste and serve immediately.

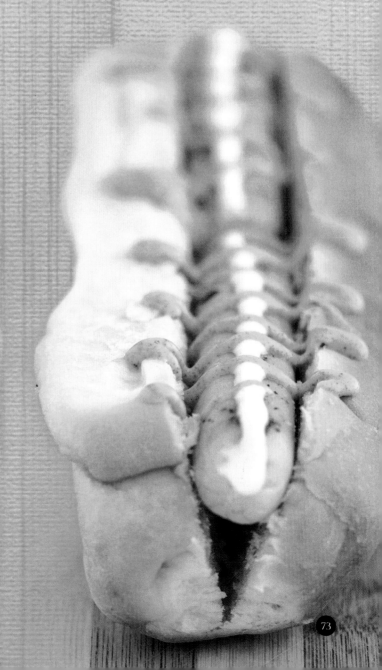

CHICKEN PITA POCKETS

Chicken finds perfect companions in mustard sauce and pita.

 Ingredients

8 (180 grams each) chicken supremes, cut in half

4 pita breads

2 medium onions, sliced

7-8 black peppercorns, crushed

2 teaspoons mustard paste

4 large lettuce leaves

2 small tomatoes, sliced

3 pickled gherkins, sliced

¼ cup Mayonnaise (page 102)

Salt to taste

2 tablespoons sesame oil

 Method

- Heat the oil in a pan and sauté the onions till translucent. Add the chicken and sauté for five minutes. Add three-fourth of the crushed peppercorns and salt and mix well.

- Heat both sides of the pita breads on a *tawa* or in an oven.

- Cut each pita bread in half, open out the pocket and apply half a teaspoon of the mustard paste inside. Arrange one lettuce leaf, some tomato slices, some chicken mixture and a few slices of gherkins in the pocket. Add some mayonnaise, sprinkle some of the remaining crushed peppercorns and salt and serve immediately.

MUSHROOM AND LEEK SPRING ROLLS

Noodles, mushrooms and leeks in a spicy and scrumptious roll!

 Ingredients

10-15 button mushrooms, sliced

8-10 shiitake mushrooms, sliced

2 leeks, sliced

10 Spring Roll Wrappers (page 25)

1 cup glass noodles

6-8 garlic cloves, chopped

1 inch ginger, chopped

5-6 black peppercorns, crushed

7-8 spring onions with greens, chopped

1 egg, beaten

Sichuan Sauce (page 102)

Salt to taste

2 tablespoons oil + for deep-frying

 Method

· Soak the glass noodles in three cups of hot water for two to three minutes. Drain thoroughly and spread on a plate to cool.

· Heat two tablespoons of oil in a wok and sauté the garlic and ginger.

· Add all the mushrooms, leeks, salt, crushed peppercorns and sauté until the moisture dries up. Remove from heat and set aside to cool. Stir in the spring onions and glass noodles.

· To assemble the rolls, place two tablespoons of the mixture in the centre of each spring roll wrapper and fold one side over the filling. Fold both the parallel sides over leaving the fourth side open. Brush the edge with some beaten egg and roll up tightly.

· Heat sufficient oil in a wok and deep-fry the spring rolls till golden brown. Drain on absorbent paper.

· Serve hot with Sichuan sauce.

SAUSAGE TRIANGLES

A variation of the samosa but very flaky...and very different!

 Ingredients

4 sheets filo pastry

200 grams chicken sausages, chopped

2 medium potatoes, boiled and mashed

1 large onion, grated

2 garlic cloves, chopped

5-6 black peppercorns, crushed

1 egg, beaten lightly

Salt to taste

3 teaspoons oil

 Method

- Preheat the oven to 220°C/425°F/Gas Mark 7.

- Heat the oil in a small pan; add the onion and garlic and sauté till translucent. Transfer to a bowl.

- Add the mashed potatoes and sausages and mix well. Add salt and the crushed peppercorns and mix again.

- Cut each pastry sheet in half. Divide the sausage mixture equally among the pastry halves, placing it at one end of the pastry sheet. Brush the beaten egg mixture around the edges and fold into triangles.

- Place the triangles on a lightly oiled baking tray. Bake, uncovered, for about twenty-five minutes, or until lightly browned. Serve hot.

Keema Roti Rolls

Succulent mince and boiled eggs in soft roti...surely encourages overeating!

 Ingredients

4 wholewheat *roti*

Filling

250 grams minced mutton

2 green chillies

½ tablespoon ginger-garlic paste

1 medium onion, chopped

1 medium tomato, chopped

2 teaspoons coriander powder

½ teaspoon turmeric powder

1 teaspoon *garam masala* powder

3 tablespoons chopped fresh coriander

1 tablespoon lemon juice

1 medium onion sliced into rings

2 hard-boiled eggs, sliced

Salt to taste

1 tablespoon oil

 Method

· Heat the oil in a pan; add the green chillies and ginger-garlic paste and sauté for half a minute. Add the onion and sauté till golden brown.

· Add the tomato, coriander powder, turmeric powder, *garam masala* powder and sauté for a few seconds.

· Add the minced mutton, mix well and sauté till all the moisture has evaporated and the mutton is cooked.

· Add the salt, fresh coriander and lemon juice. Divide into four portions.

· Place one portion of minced mutton on each *roti* and top it with a few onion rings and egg slices. Roll up firmly to enclose the mutton completely.

· Serve hot.

CHILLI-CHICKEN CROISSANTS

There is something therapeutic about baking croissants: maybe the procedure means a lot of busy activity that's why!

Ingredients

Croissant

4 cups refined flour + for dusting

2½ tablespoons milk powder

2 teaspoons salt

1 tablespoon fresh yeast

3 tablespoons sugar

1¼ cups butter

1 egg, beaten

Filling

200 grams chicken fillets, roughly chopped

150 grams chicken salami, roughly chopped

1 garlic clove, finely chopped

1 small onion, chopped

1 teaspoon paprika

½ teaspoon oregano

2 tablespoons finely chopped fresh coriander

2 stalks spring onion greens, finely chopped

Salt to taste

1 tablespoon oil

Method

- In a bowl, mix together four cups of flour, milk powder and salt. Dissolve yeast and sugar in half cup of warm water and allow it to stand for fifteen minutes. Keep butter in deep freezer for chilling.

- Add the yeast mixture to the flour. Add three-fourth cup water and knead into a smooth dough. Keep the dough, covered with a damp muslin, in a warm place to rise for thirty to forty minutes.

- Slice the chilled butter into thin slices.

- Knock back the dough and roll into a forty centimetre by seventy centimetre rectangle using a little flour for dusting. Brush off the excess flour.

- Arrange the chilled butter on two-thirds of the rectangle in the centre. Fold the uncovered one-third part over to the centre and bring over the remaining one-third part to make a book fold. Seal the sides well so that the butter does not come out.

- Roll the pastry again to the same size and make a book fold. Keep in the refrigerator for half an hour covered in cling film so that no moisture goes in.

- Repeat the process twice without the butter. Again roll the dough into a rectangle of the same size and trim the sides.

- For the filling, heat oil in a pan and sauté the garlic and onion till translucent. Add the chicken fillets and salami and stir-fry till chicken is cooked but still juicy. Add salt, paprika, oregano, fresh coriander and spring onion greens and toss. Set aside.

- Cut the rectangular dough into two strips, lengthwise, with a sharp knife. Further cut into large triangles with each side measuring approximately fifteen centimetres.

- Place the triangles on a lightly floured surface. Place one tablespoon of chicken mixture at the base of the triangle. Roll it in the shape of a crescent.

- Arrange on a baking tray, lightly brush with the beaten egg and leave to rise in a warm, humid place for thirty minutes or till doubled in size.

- Preheat the oven to 200°C/400°F/Gas Mark 6.

- Bake the croissants in the preheated oven for fifteen minutes. Reduce the temperature to 190°C/375°F/Gas Mark 5 and further bake for ten minutes. Serve hot.

CHICKEN ROLLS

Kids being fussy? Fill their plates with this and watch it being demolished in minutes!

Ingredients

2 (250 grams) chicken breasts, boiled and shredded

4 hot dog rolls

½ cup Mayonnaise (page 102)

1 garlic clove, chopped

1 tablespoon tomato ketchup

1 tablespoon mustard paste

Black pepper powder to taste

A few lettuce leaves, to garnish

Salt to taste

Method

- Place the mayonnaise, garlic, tomato ketchup, mustard paste, salt, pepper powder and shredded chicken in a bowl and mix well. Divide into four portions.

- Slit the hot dog rolls but do not cut through.

- Line the rolls with lettuce leaves and spread one portion of the chicken mixture on the bottom half of each roll and press the top half down lightly. Secure with a toothpick and serve immediately.

Omelette Rolls With Sprouts And Sev

Eggs are versatile, but this recipe will always be counted as ingenious.

 Ingredients

8 eggs

1 cup mixed sprouts, blanched

¼ cup *sev*

3 medium onions

2 garlic cloves, chopped

1 small green capsicum, cut into thin strips

¼ teaspoon mixed dried herbs

¼ teaspoon red chilli flakes

3-4 black peppercorns, crushed

4 green chillies, finely chopped

Salt to taste

5 tablespoons oil

 Method

- Slice one onion and finely chop the remaining two.

- Heat one tablespoon of oil in a pan. Add the garlic and sliced onion and sauté till translucent. Add the capsicum and sauté for a minute. Add the sprouts, dried herbs, chilli flakes, crushed peppercorns and salt and mix well. Divide the mixture into four portions.

- Break two eggs in a bowl, add salt and beat well.

- Heat one tablespoon of oil in a non-stick pan; add a portion of the chopped onions and green chillies and sauté for one minute.

- Add the beaten eggs, stir and rotate the pan so that the eggs spread evenly. Let the underside cook for a minute. Flip over and cook again for a minute.

- Place the sprouts mixture on one side and top it with sev. Fold the other side over or roll up and serve immediately.

- Similarly prepare the other omelette rolls from the remaining eggs.

MINCE HOT DOG ROLLS

Tender chicken kababs in a soft roll...a delight for kids and adults alike.

 Ingredients

350 grams minced chicken

4 hot dog rolls

1 tablespoon ginger-garlic-green chilli paste

2 tablespoons cashew nut paste

1 teaspoon *chaat masala*

1 teaspoon *garam masala* powder

1 teaspoon white pepper powder

4 tablespoons chopped fresh coriander

1 tablespoon lemon juice

2 tablespoons butter

1 head of lettuce, shredded

2 medium onions, chopped

4 tablespoons Mint Chutney (page 102)

Salt to taste

2 tablespoons oil

 Method

- Place the minced chicken in a bowl. Add the ginger-garlic-green chilli paste, cashew nut paste, *chaat masala*, *garam masala* powder, pepper powder, fresh coriander, lemon juice and salt. Mix well and divide into four portions.

- Moisten your hands, take each portion of the chicken mixture and press it firmly around a satay stick.

- Heat a *tawa* and drizzle some oil on it. Place the satay sticks on the *tawa* and cook, turning them from time to time so that they cook evenly on all sides. Baste the *kababs* with butter at regular intervals. Remove when completely cooked and set aside.

- Heat another *tawa*. Slit the hot dog rolls without cutting through and roast them on the *tawa* till slightly crisp.

- Place some lettuce on each hot dog roll. Place a *kabab* on the lettuce and top it with some onions and mint chutney.

- Press the top of the roll down lightly and serve immediately.

SEEKH ROTI

Good as a snack, even better as dinner.

 Ingredients

 Method

For the filling

500 grams boneless mutton, cut into 1-inch cubes

4 tablespoons unripe green papaya paste

1 tablespoon garlic paste

½ tablespoon ginger paste

4-5 green chillies, chopped

1 tablespoon red chilli powder

½ tablespoon coriander powder

1 teaspoon roasted cumin powder

1 teaspoon *garam masala* powder

2 large onions, chopped

1 teaspoon poppy seeds

1 teaspoon sesame seeds

1½ tablespoons vinegar

Salt to taste

3 tablespoons *ghee*

To serve

8 *roomali roti*

¼ cup Green Chutney (page 102)

2 large onions, sliced

2 tablespoons chopped fresh mint

- In a large bowl, combine the mutton, papaya paste, garlic paste, ginger paste, green chillies, chilli powder, coriander powder, roasted cumin powder, *garam masala* powder and salt. Leave to marinate for four to five hours, preferably in a refrigerator.

- Heat two tablespoons *ghee* in a *kadai*; add the onion and sauté over medium heat till pale gold.

- Add the marinated mutton, stir and cook, uncovered, on low heat for ten minutes. Add half a cup of water, cover and cook for twenty to twenty-five minutes or till the mutton is tender.

- Add the poppy and sesame seeds and continue to cook, uncovered, for another fifteen minutes till all the water has evaporated. Stir in the vinegar, remove from heat and set aside.

- To obtain a smoky flavour, place a live piece of charcoal in a bowl and place the bowl in the centre of the mutton mixture. Pour one tablespoon of hot *ghee* on the charcoal, cover the pan immediately and leave to stand for three to four minutes. Remove the bowl with the charcoal from the mutton mixture.

- To prepare the wraps, divide the mutton mixture into eight equal portions. Place a *roti* on a plate and smear some green chutney over it. Spread a portion of the mutton mixture over the *roti*, sprinkle some sliced onions and fresh mint, roll up into a wrap and secure with a piece of aluminium foil.

Note: Roomali roti can be replaced with large, thin wholewheat roti.

SHAWARMA

Fast food staple in the Middle East, this is becoming popular worldwide. Now in a few easy steps make it at home.

 Ingredients

4 (180 grams each) chicken breasts

4 pita breads

Salt to taste

4 tablespoons olive oil

Yogurt sauce

1 cup yogurt

1 teaspoon garlic paste

2 tablespoons lemon juice

1 sprig fresh parsley

Salt to taste

Salad

1 medium onion, sliced

1 medium tomato, sliced

2 jalapeño chillies, sliced

2 tablespoons *tahini*

3 tablespoons yogurt

6-8 fresh mint, roughly torn

Salt to taste

 Method

- For the yogurt sauce, add the salt and garlic paste to the yogurt and whisk well. Stir in the lemon juice. Spoon the mixture into a piece of muslin (*malmal*) placed over a bowl, gather the edges and squeeze tightly to get a thick, smooth yogurt sauce. Garnish with a sprig of parsley and set aside.

- Preheat the oven to 200°C/400°F/ Gas Mark 6.

- Slit the chicken breasts lengthways without cutting through. Drizzle olive oil over them, sprinkle salt and thread them in folds onto a skewer. Place the skewer on a rotisserie (rotating rack). Place the rotisserie in the preheated oven and cook for twenty minutes.

- Remove from the oven and slice the chicken into thin pieces while still on the skewer.

- Toast the pita breads lightly on a *tawa* or in an oven. Slit them open to form pockets.

- For the salad mix together the onion, tomato, jalapeños, salt, tahini, yogurt and fresh mint.

- Stuff the pita pocket with some of the sliced chicken mixture and top with the onion-tomato salad.

- Serve immediately with the yogurt sauce.

Moussaka Crêpes

Want a Mediterranean feel to your supper? This is really elaborate so you can dish it up for those special occasions.

 Ingredients

 Method

Crêpes

½ cup refined flour

1 egg

1 tablespoon butter + for greasing

1 cup milk

1 cup Cheese Sauce (page 102)

Filling

1 small brinjal, diced

250 grams minced mutton

4 tablespoons butter

6 shallots

½ teaspoon dried oregano

1 garlic clove, crushed

2 tomatoes, blanched, peeled and chopped

2 teaspoons tomato paste

Black pepper powder to taste

½ cup fresh breadcrumbs

2 tablespoons grated Parmesan cheese

Salt to taste

2 tablespoons oil

- For the crêpes, sift the refined flour into a bowl. Add the egg, one tablespoon melted butter and two tablespoons of milk. Beat until smooth. Add the remaining milk a little by little to make a smooth batter. Set aside for thirty minutes.

- Heat a non-stick frying pan over medium heat; lightly grease it with butter and pour two-three tablespoons of batter into the pan. Rotate the pan so that the batter spreads all around.

- Cook over low heat until the batter has set and lightly browned underneath. Turn and brown the other side as well. Remove the crêpe and set aside on a plate. Repeat with the remaining batter. Keep the crêpes warm.

- Preheat the oven to 180°C/350°F/Gas Mark 4.

- For the filling, sprinkle the brinjal pieces with one teaspoon salt and set aside for thirty minutes. Rinse under cold water and drain on absorbent paper.

- Heat the oil in pan; add the minced mutton and sauté for ten minutes. Remove from the pan and set aside.

- Melt the butter in the same pan. Add the brinjal, shallots, oregano and garlic and cook for one minute. Add the tomatoes, tomato paste and pepper powder and cook for one minute. Transfer to a bowl and add the sautéed lamb, the breadcrumbs, Parmesan cheese and half a cup of cheese sauce. Mix thoroughly and adjust the seasoning.

- Place two tablespoons of filling at one end of each crêpe and roll up, tucking in the sides.

- Arrange the crêpes in a shallow eleven-inch square ovenproof dish. Pour the remaining cheese sauce over and bake, uncovered, for fifteen minutes. Remove from the oven and serve warm.

SEAFOOD SPRING ROLLS

The presentation is impressive, so is the filling! So, count this in as one of those 'specialities'.

 Ingredients

½ cup peeled shrimps

2 (200-250 grams) pomfret fillets cut into 1-inch pieces

½ cup clams

4 Spring Roll Wrappers (page 25)

2 eggs

2 inches ginger, finely chopped

1 teaspoon sesame oil

½ cup thinly sliced spring onions

¼ cup chopped fresh coriander

10-12 black peppercorns, crushed

Salt to taste

Oil for deep-frying

 Method

· To make the filling, combine the shrimps, pomfret, clams, one egg, ginger and sesame oil in a food processor and chop finely. Transfer to a large bowl and mix in the spring onions and fresh coriander. Season with salt and crushed peppercorns.

· Beat the other egg with one-fourth cup of water to make an egg wash.

· For the rolls, place some of the seafood mixture a little below one corner of a spring roll wrapper. Bring in the corners to enclose the filling. Brush the edges with the egg wash, roll tightly towards the middle.

· Heat sufficient oil in a wok. Deep-fry the rolls till golden brown. Drain on absorbent paper.

· Cut the rolls diagonally into two and serve with Sichuan Sauce (page 102).

MUTTON FRANKIES

Top of the rolls, frankies always win over the fussy eater.

 Ingredients

 Method

350 grams boneless mutton, cut into ½-inch thin pieces

1½ cups refined flour

3 large onions

2 teaspoons ginger paste

2 teaspoons garlic paste

2 teaspoons coriander powder

½ teaspoon turmeric powder

2 teaspoons red chilli powder

2 large tomatoes, chopped

2 tablespoons fresh coriander, finely chopped

½ teaspoon *garam masala* powder

3 eggs, beaten

4 teaspoons chilli vinegar

Salt to taste

2 tablespoons oil

- Roughly chop two onions and slice the remaining one.

- Mix the refined flour and salt in a bowl. Add sufficient water and knead into a soft dough.

- Heat two tablespoons of oil in a pressure cooker. Add the roughly chopped onion and sauté for two minutes. Add the ginger paste, garlic paste and continue to sauté for another minute.

- Add the mutton pieces and sauté for two to three minutes. Add the salt, coriander powder, turmeric powder and chilli powder and mix.

- Add the tomatoes and sauté for two to three minutes. Add a quarter cup of water. When the mixture comes to a boil, close the lid of the pressure cooker and cook under pressure till the pressure is released five or six times (five or six whistles).

- Remove the lid when the pressure has reduced completely. Stir in the fresh coriander and *garam masala* powder and cook till the mixture is dry.

- Divide the dough into eight equal portions and roll out into *roti*. Cook each *roti*, on a hot *tawa* till almost done.

- Pour some beaten egg over the *roti* and cook till set. Turn over to cook the other side.

- Place the *roti*, egg side up, on a serving plate. Place some of the mutton mixture at one end. Sprinkle some onion over the mutton. Drizzle some chilli vinegar and roll up firmly. Serve immediately.

Mawa Rolls

I love to call this malpua's distant cousin! Don't count calories when it is served…just enjoy it!

 Ingredients

Pancakes

1 cup refined flour

A pinch of salt

½ teaspoon baking powder

½ teaspoon soda bicarbonate

1½ tablespoons powdered sugar

¼ cup *khoya/mawa*, grated

1 cup milk

Ghee for greasing

Filling

800 grams *khoya/mawa*, grated

¼ cup milk

10 tablespoons powdered sugar

1½ teaspoons green cardamom powder

50 pistachios, roughly chopped

50 almonds, roughly chopped

 Method

· For the pancakes, sieve refined flour, salt, baking powder, soda bicarbonate and sugar in a bowl. Add the grated *khoya* and mix. Add milk and mix well. Ensure that there are no lumps. Adjust the consistency by adding more milk.

· Heat the *ghee* in a pan. Pour a ladleful of the batter and spread to a medium thickness. Cook till done on one side then flip and cook on the other side. Transfer onto a plate and set aside.

· For the filling, heat a *kadai*, add grated *khoya*, milk and powdered sugar and cook till soft. Add cardamom powder, pistachios and almonds and mix. Take the mixture off the heat.

· Place a pancake on a plate. Spread a little of the filling and roll. Make more rolls with the remaining batter and filling.

· Cut the rolls diagonally in the middle and serve hot.

Swiss Rolls

A teatime delight, it is also an eternal favourite with the sweet-toothed.

Ingredients

¾ cup refined flour

½ teaspoon baking powder

4 eggs, separated

¾ cup powdered sugar, sifted

1 teaspoon vanilla essence

¼ teaspoon salt

2 teaspoons caster sugar, for dusting

5 tablespoons mixed fruit jam

Method

· Preheat the oven to 190°C/375°F/Gas Mark 5. Line a fifteen-inch by ten-inch baking tray with greased thick, unglazed brown paper.

· Sift the flour with baking powder. Beat the egg yolks until light. Continue beating the mixture, adding the sugar gradually, till creamy. Stir in the vanilla essence. Gently and gradually fold in the flour into the egg mixture. Beat the batter until smooth. Whip the egg whites with salt until stiff, but not dry. Fold in the egg whites lightly into the batter.

· Spread the batter in the prepared tray and bake for about twelve minutes.

· While still hot, turn the cake out onto a sheet of greaseproof paper, sprinkled with caster sugar. Trim the hard edges. Spread the jam on the cake and carefully roll it up. Wrap the roll in the greaseproof paper.

· Allow to rest for half-an-hour. Remove the paper gently. Cut the cake into slices and serve.

BOONDI AND RABDI-STUFFED PANCAKES

Heavy-duty dessert! You can substitute the laddoos with sweet boondi if you desire.

 Ingredients

6 medium *boondi laddoos*

3-4 tablespoons *rabdi* + to serve

1½ cups refined flour

1 teaspoon baking powder

1 teaspoon soda bicarbonate

¾ cup buttermilk

2 tablespoons powdered sugar

1 tablespoon raisins

 Method

· Preheat the oven to 180°C/350°F/Gas Mark 4.

· Sieve refined flour, baking powder and soda bicarbonate into a bowl. Add buttermilk and whisk to make a smooth batter. Add powdered sugar and mix.

· Heat a non-stick pan. Pour a ladleful of batter and spread it around. Cook till the underside is lightly browned. Flip and cook till the other side is cooked similarly. Transfer onto a plate and set aside. Cook other pancakes similarly.

· Take *boondi laddoos* in a bowl and break them. Add raisins and three to four tablespoons of *rabdi* and mix.

· Take a springform cake tin. Trim the pancakes to fit into the tin.

· Keep one pancake at the base of the tin. Spread some of the *boondi* stuffing over it. Cover with another pancake and spread some more of the stuffing. Keep another pancake and spread some more of the stuffing.

· Keep the tin in the preheated oven and bake for ten minutes.

· Remove from the oven and unmould. Cut into wedges and serve with *rabdi*.

OAT PANCAKES WITH DRIED FRUIT

Breakfast idea, better for brunch! For added style, cook in a waffle iron and sandwich the filling between two waffles.

 Ingredients

⅛ cup oatmeal

¼ cup refined flour

¼ cup wholewheat flour

A pinch of soda bicarbonate

A pinch of baking powder

1 tablespoon powdered sugar

1½ eggs

½ cup buttermilk

⅛ cup milk

A few drops of vanilla essence

1 tablespoon oil + for shallow-frying

Filling

2 tablespoons butter

½ cup dates, chopped

15 cashew nuts, chopped

15 pistachios, chopped

15 almonds, chopped

¾ cup maple syrup

 Method

- Sift together both types of flour, soda bicarbonate and baking powder into a bowl.

- Add the powdered sugar and mix. Add the eggs and mix again. Add the buttermilk and mix well to make a smooth batter.

- Add oatmeal and milk and mix. Add a little oil and vanilla essence and mix well.

- To make the filling, melt butter in a pan and toss all the dried fruit in it for two to three minutes. Transfer into a bowl and let it cool a bit. Add maple syrup and mix.

- Heat a pan, grease it with a little oil. Pour a ladleful of batter and spread evenly on the pan. Drizzle a little oil all round and let it cook on medium heat for two minutes. Flip and cook on the other side.

- Place a little of the filling on one side of the pancake and roll it up.

- Serve hot.

CHOCOLATE PANCAKES WITH EXOTIC FRUIT

Wonderful way to introduce fruits to fussy kids...the chocolate is a great lure.

 Ingredients

Pancake

100 grams chocolate

1 tablespoon cocoa powder

¾ cup refined flour

1 cup warm milk

1 egg

Filling

1 small apple, cut into ½-inch cubes

2 small bananas, cut into ½-inch cubes

1 kiwi fruit, cut into ½-inch cubes

1 tablespoon butter

¼ cup caster sugar

2 tablespoons port wine/fruit juice

¼ cup pomegranate kernels

 Method

- For the pancake batter, place the chocolate in a heatproof bowl and melt it in a double boiler. Once it cools slightly, add warm milk and egg and mix gently. Add cocoa powder and flour and whisk till smooth. Chill the batter in the refrigerator for thirty minutes.

- For the filling, heat the butter in a pan. When it melts add caster sugar and mix well.

- Add the fruit cubes, port wine or fruit juice. Lower the heat and simmer till fruits are tender and totally dry. Add pomegranate kernels and mix well. Remove the pan from heat and keep warm.

- To make the pancakes, heat a non-stick pan, pour in just enough batter to cover the base of the pan and swirl to coat evenly. Cook till pancake sets and flip it to cook the other side. Gently slide the pancake onto a plate.

- Divide the filling into as many portions as the number of pancakes. Place a pancake on a plate, spread fruit mixture on one half and fold the other half over.

- Serve immediately.

CINNAMON ROLLS

My favourite with a cup of hot cappuccino! Do try it!

 Ingredients

 Method

Dough

4 cups refined flour

2¼ teaspoons yeast

1/3 cup sugar

2 eggs

1/3 cup butter, melted

½ cup sour cream

1 teaspoon vanilla essence

Salt to taste

Oil to grease

Filling

2 teaspoons
cinnamon powder

1 cup brown sugar

1 teaspoon nutmeg powder

3 tablespoons soft butter +
for greasing

½ cup raisins

½ cup walnuts, chopped

- Place yeast and one teaspoon of sugar in a mixing bowl. Add a quarter cup warm water and stir. Let the mixture stand for five to ten minutes or until it is frothy.

- Add the remaining sugar, eggs, butter, sour cream, vanilla essence and salt. Mix well. Add two cups of flour and mix well. Stir in the remaining flour, one fourth cup at a time, until the dough sticks together but is not dry.

- Place the dough on a lightly floured surface. Knead for about five minutes, or until the dough is smooth. Grease a bowl, place the dough in it, coat it with a little oil, cover with a cling film or damp towel and place in a warm place for about one-and-a-half hours or till it doubles in volume.

- Beat back the dough with your fists. Place it back on the floured surface and knead for one minute. Cover the dough with a towel and let it rest till the filling is ready.

- For the filling, mix together the cinnamon, brown sugar and nutmeg powder in a small bowl.

- Lightly dust the rolling pin with flour and roll the dough into a rectangle about thirty by sixty centimetres. Spread three tablespoons butter all over the dough. Sprinkle the sugar mixture, raisins and nuts. Press the nuts and raisins lightly into the dough with the back of a wooden spoon.

- Starting at the narrow end, roll the dough as tightly as you can towards the other end. Pinch the seam to seal it. Cut the roll diagonally into twelve equal pieces.

- Grease a baking tray well with butter. Arrange the pieces, cut side down, in the tray. Cover tightly with a plastic wrap. Place in a warm place for about one-and-a-half hours or till the pieces double in size.

- Preheat oven to 150°C/300°F/Gas Mark 2. Bake the rolls in the preheated oven for thirty minutes or until golden brown.

- Serve hot or at room temperature.

ANNEXURE

 Cheese Sauce

Melt 2 tablespoons of butter in a pan; add 2 tablespoons of refined flour and cook over low heat for a few minutes. Gradually stir in 2 cups of warm milk, and stir continuously till thick. Stir in 1 cup of grated cheese, white pepper powder and salt to taste. Cook till the cheese melts.

 Sichuan Sauce

Boil 10-12 dried red chillies in one cup of water for five to seven minutes. Drain, cool and grind to a fine paste. Heat ½ cup oil in a pan and add 10 garlic cloves, peeled and finely chopped, 2 finely chopped green chillies, 2 finely chopped spring onions and 1-inch peeled and grated ginger. Sauté for a minute, then add the red chilli paste and sauté a bit more. Add a 2-3 inch celery stalk, 3 tablespoons tomato ketchup and salt to taste. Stir well to mix. Stir in 2 teaspoons white vinegar and simmer for a minute. Take the pan off the heat when the oil rises to the surface. Cool and store. Sichuan sauce will keep for a month if there is sufficient oil covering the surface.

 Green Chutney

Grind together 1 cup fresh coriander, ½ cup fresh mint, 2-3 green chillies, black salt to taste, ¼ teaspoon sugar and 1 tablespoon lemon juice to a smooth paste using a little water if required.

 Mint Chutney

Grind 5 cups fresh mint, 3 cups fresh coriander, 10 green chillies, 3 onions, and 3 inches of ginger to a fine paste, adding a little water if required. Stir in 1 tablespoon lemon juice, salt and pomegranate seed powder.

 Mayonnaise

Place 1 egg yolk, salt to taste, ¼ teaspoon each white pepper powder, mustard powder and sugar and 1 teaspoon vinegar in a clean bowl and mix thoroughly with a whisk. Alternatively, process the mixture in a blender. Add 1 cup of oil, a little at a time, whisking or blending continuously, until all the oil is incorporated. Add 1 teaspoon lemon juice and adjust seasoning. Store in an airtight jar in a refrigerator.

GLOSSARY

ENGLISH	HINDI	ENGLISH	HINDI
Almonds	badam	Cornflour	makai ka atta
Apple	seb	Cottage cheese	paneer
Banana	kela	Cucumber	kakdi
Bean curd	tofu	Cumin seeds	jeera
Bean sprouts	ankurit moong	Crab meat	kekde ka maas
Black grapes	kale angoor	Dried fenugreek leaves	kasoori methi
Black peppercorns	kali mirch	Dried mango powder	amchur
Black sesame seeds	kala til	Dried yeast	sookha khameer
Boneless mutton	gosht ki boti	Eggplants	baingan
Bread crumbs	bread ka choora	Eggs	ande
Brinjal	baingan	Fenugreek seeds	methi
Butter	makhkhan	French beans	farsi
Buttermilk	chaas	Fresh basil	tulsi ke patte
Button mushrooms	kukurmutta	Fresh coriander	hara dhania
Cabbage	patta gobhi	Fresh cream (dairy)	malai
Caraway seeds	shahi jeera	Fresh mint	pudina
Carrot	gajar	Fresh spinach leaves	palak
Cashewnuts	kaju	Fresh yeast	taza khameer
Caster sugar	pisi hui cheeni	Garlic cloves	lehsun ki kaliyan
Cauliflower	phoolgobhi	Gherkin	kheera
Celery	ajmoda	Ginger	adrak
Chicken breasts	murg ka seena	Gram flour	besan
Chicken mince	keema	Green capsicum	hari Shimla mirch
Cinnamon	dalchini	Green chillies	hari mirch
Clams	shevma	Green peas	matar
Cloves	lavang		
Coriander seeds	dhania		

ENGLISH	HINDI	ENGLISH	HINDI
Honey	shahad	Red chilli	lal mirch
Lemons	nimboo	Red kidney beans	rajma
Lettuce leaves	salad ke patte	Refined flour	maida
Milk	doodh	Roasted peanuts	bhuni moongphali
Minced chicken	murgh ka keema	Sago	sabudana
Minced mutton	gosht ka keema	Salt	namak
Molasses	khaand	Semolina	rawa/sooji
Mushrooms	kukurmutta	Sesame oil	til ka tel
Mustard	rai	Sesame seeds	til
Nutmeg powder	jaiphal ka powder	Shrimps	chhote jheenge
Oatmeal	jau ka atta	Soda bicarbonate	meetha namak/ khane ka soda
Oil	tel	Spring onions	hara pyaaz
Olive oil	jaitun ka tel	Sugar	cheeni
Onions	pyaaz	Sweetcorn	makai ke daane
Peanut oil	moongphali ka tel	Tahini (sesame seed paste)	pisa hua til
Pineapple	ananas	Tomato	tamatar
Pine nuts	chilgoze	Turmeric	haldi
Pistachios	pista		
Pomegranate kernels	anar ke daane	Vinegar/White vinegar/Balsamic vinegar	sirka
Pomegranate seeds, dried	anardana	Walnuts	akhrot
Poppy seeds	khuskhus	Water chestnuts	shingada
Potatoes	aloo	White sesame seeds	safed til
Powdered sugar	pisi hui cheeni	Whole dry red chillies	sookhi lal mirch
Prawns	jheenga	Wholewheat flour	atta
Raisins	kishmish	Yellow capsicums	pili Shimla mirch
Red cabbage	lal patta gobhi	Yogurt	dahi
Red capsicum	lal Shimla mirch		

Sanjeev Kapoor's

WRAP N ROLL

PopulaR
prakashan

...arprakashan.com